9am
800' asl

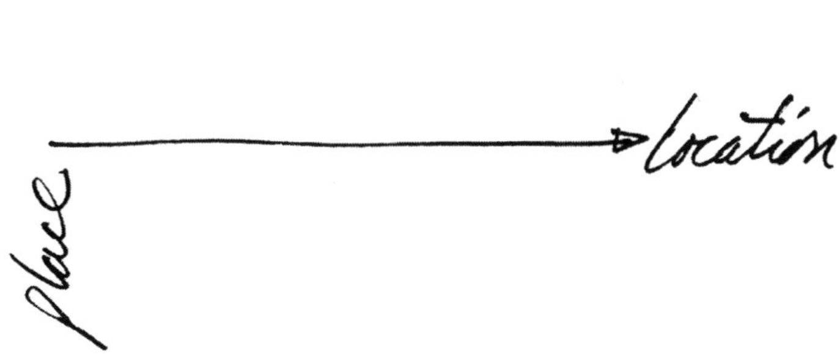
location
place

Vertical locative

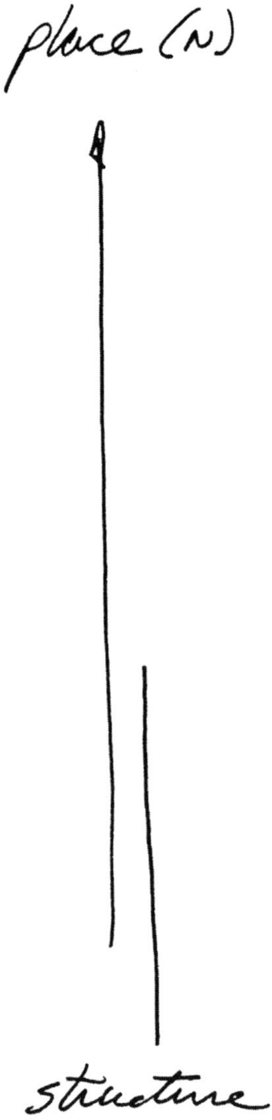

horizontal

→ here

zone – interior
exterior

vertical

where – locative

now

here

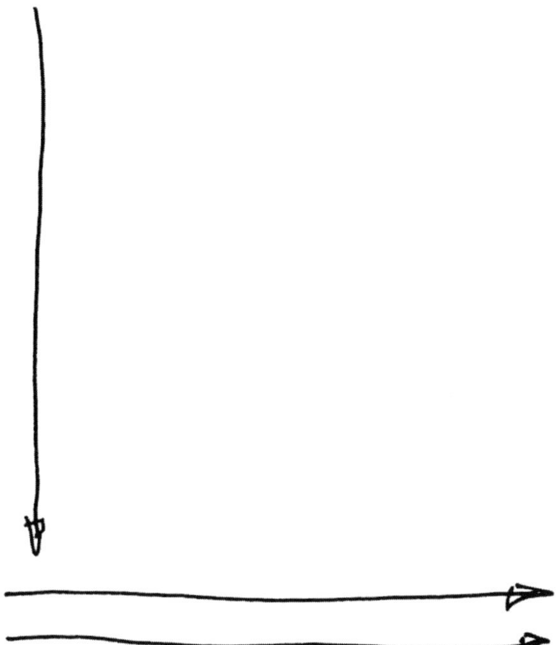

au
depart

where (location)

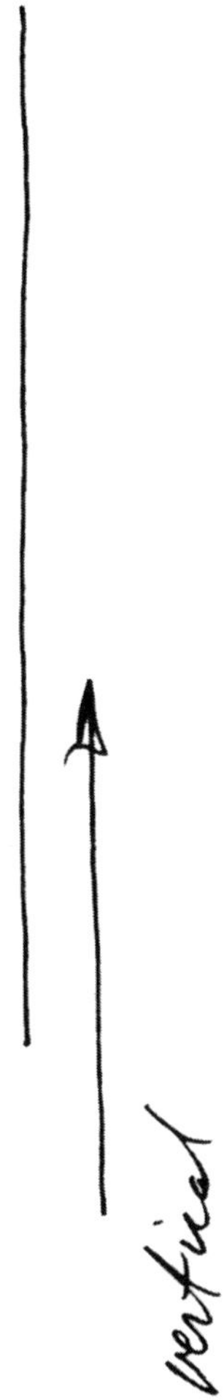

horizontal

here

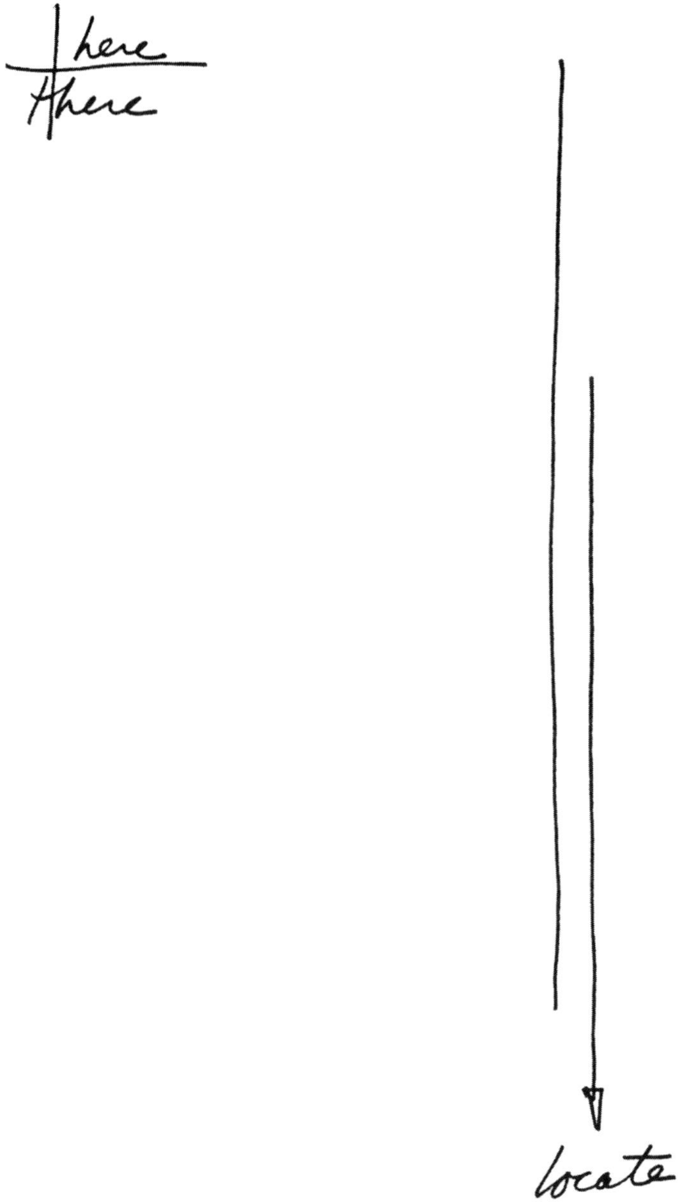
here
there
locate

there – locative

here

open
close

there → up

now → down

apart
depart

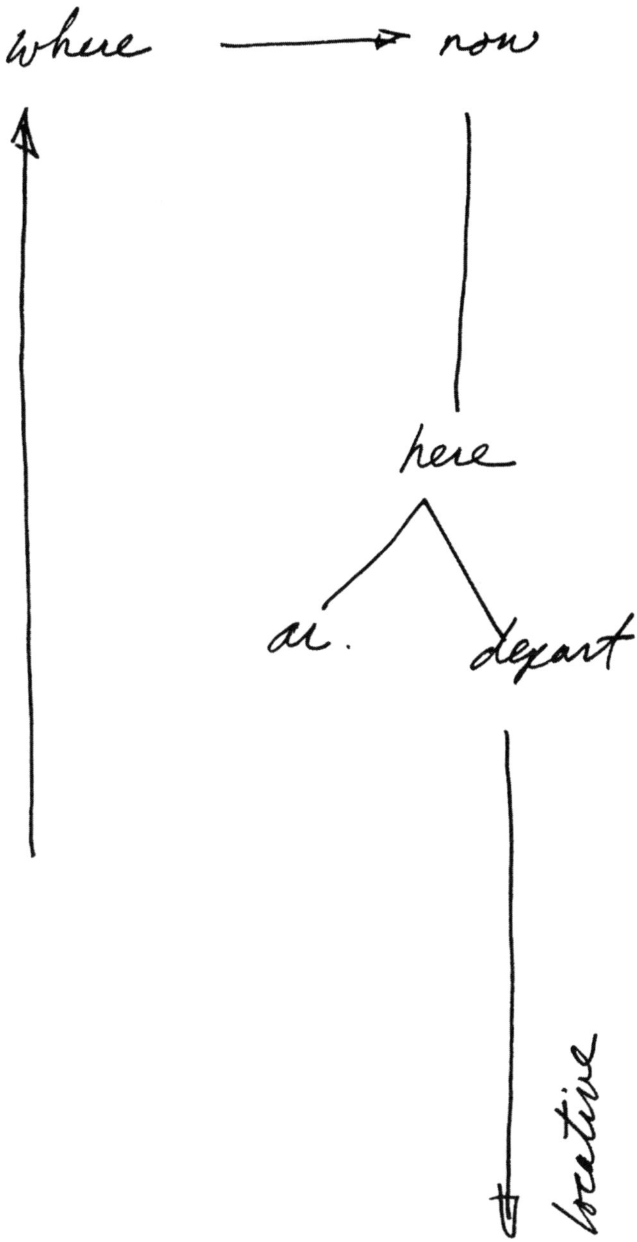
where
now
here
ai.
depart
locative

where | here
there

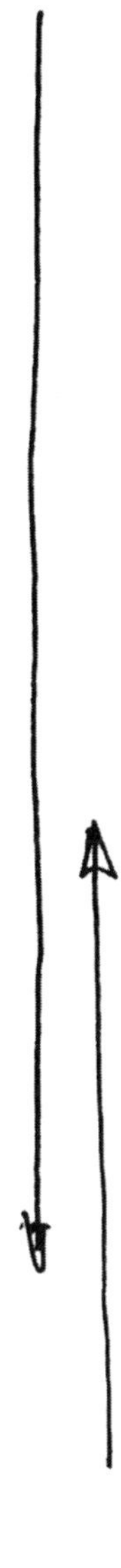

ar.
depart

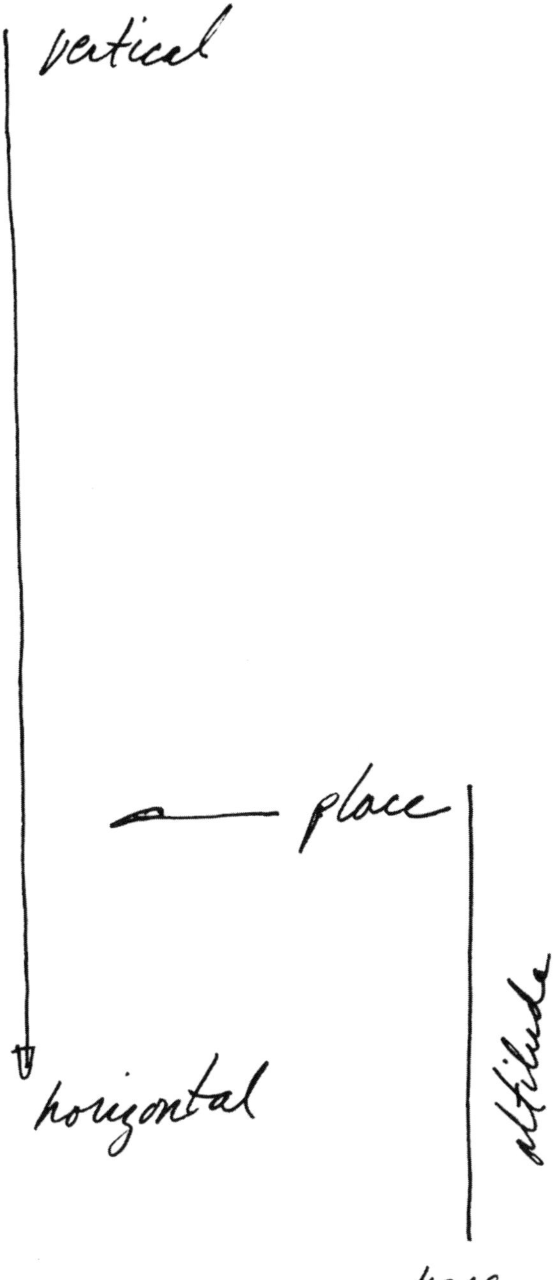
vertical
place
horizontal
altitude
here

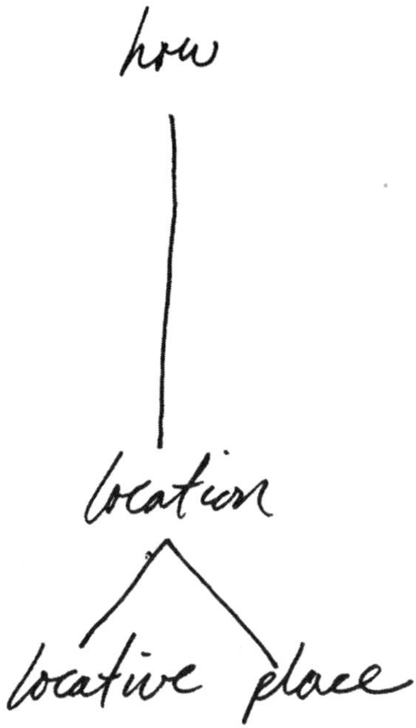

interior
exterior

here

there

locate

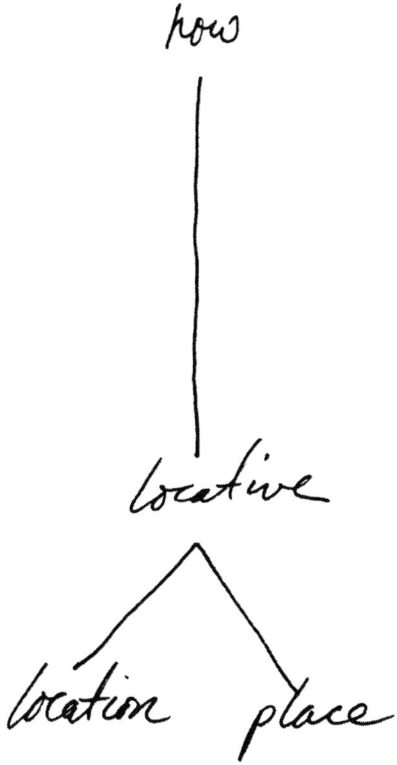
now
locative
location
place

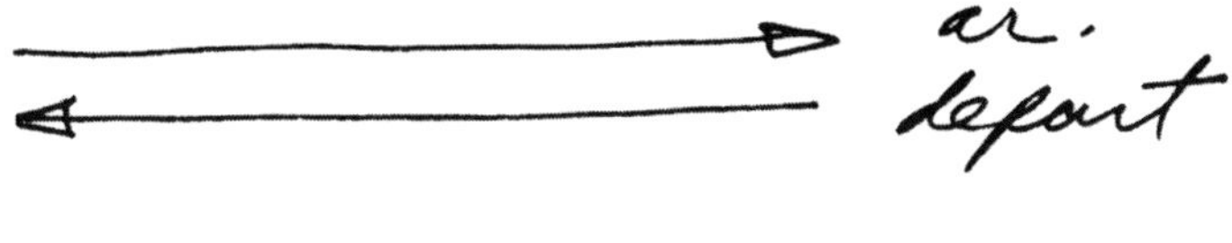
ar.
depart

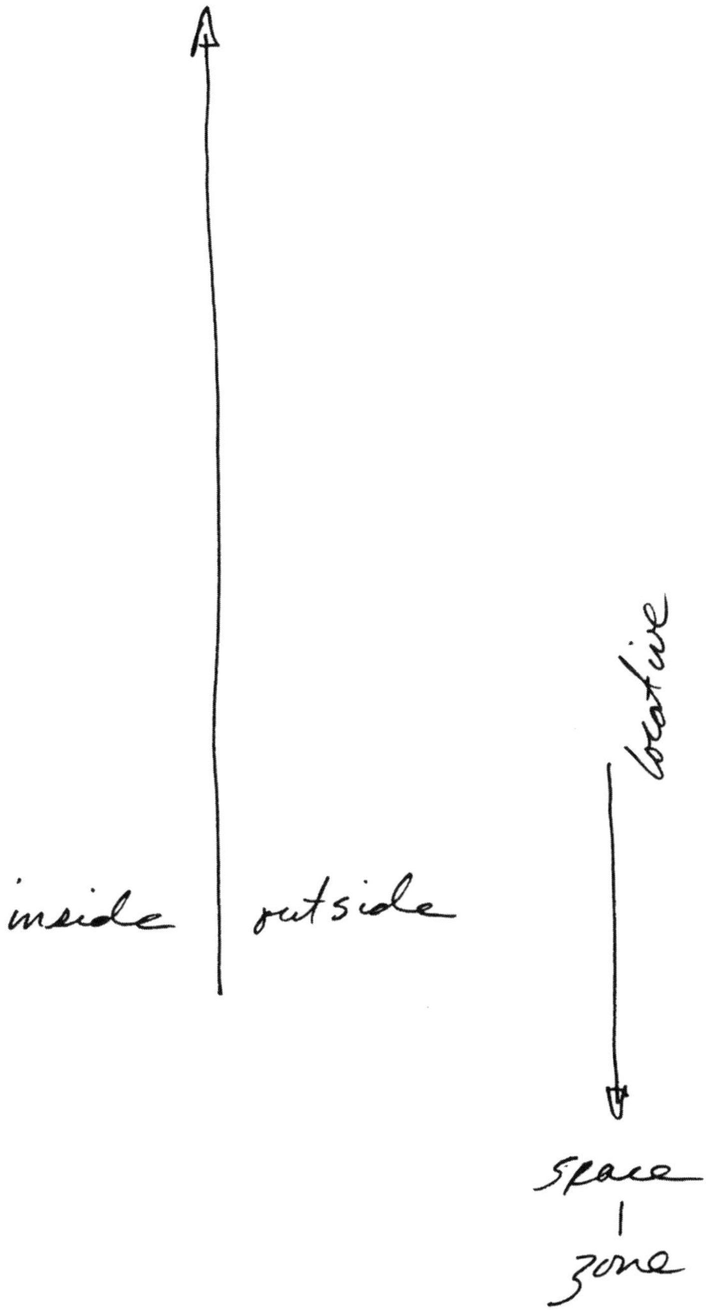
inside
outside
locative
space
zone

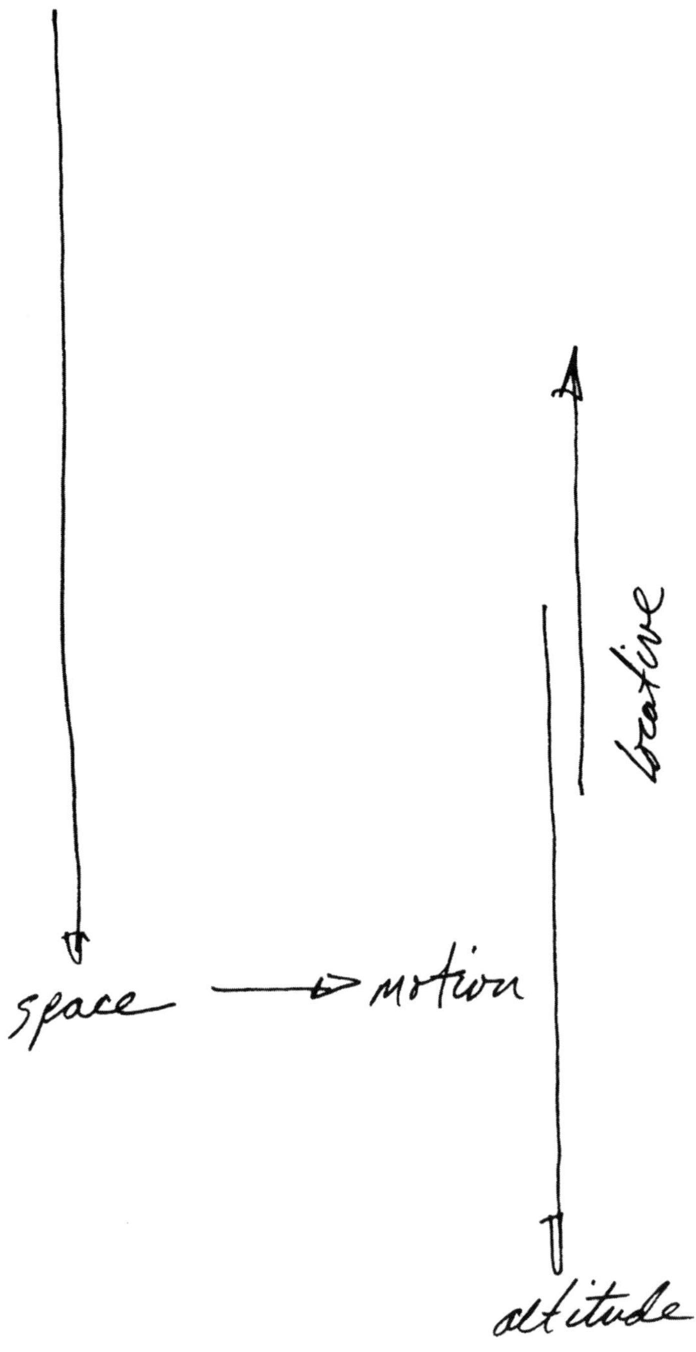
space
motion
locative
altitude

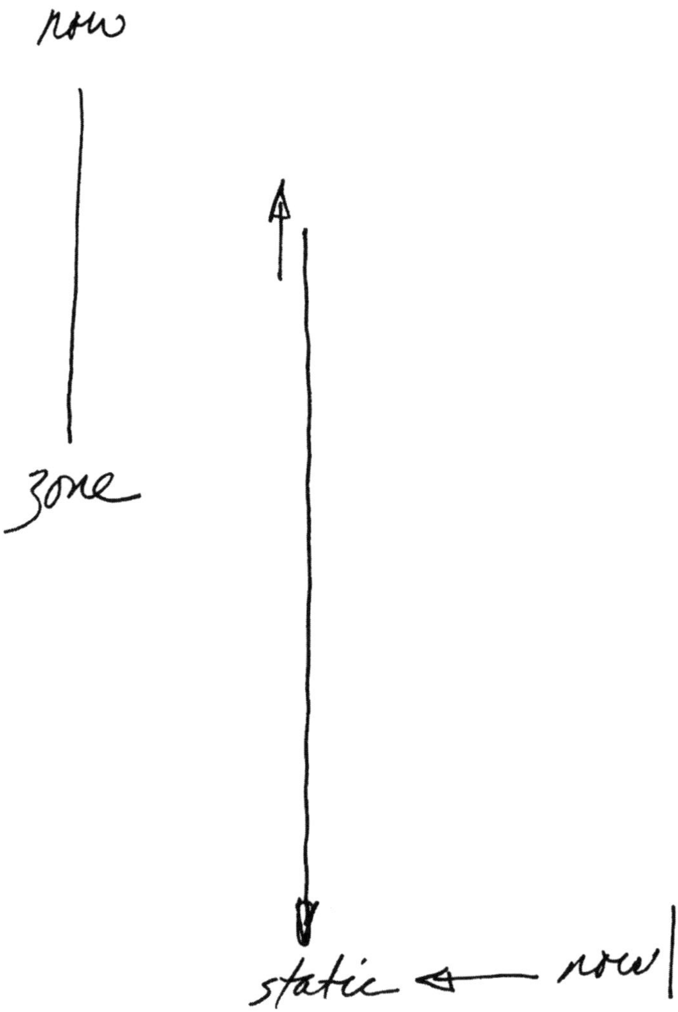
now
zone
static
now

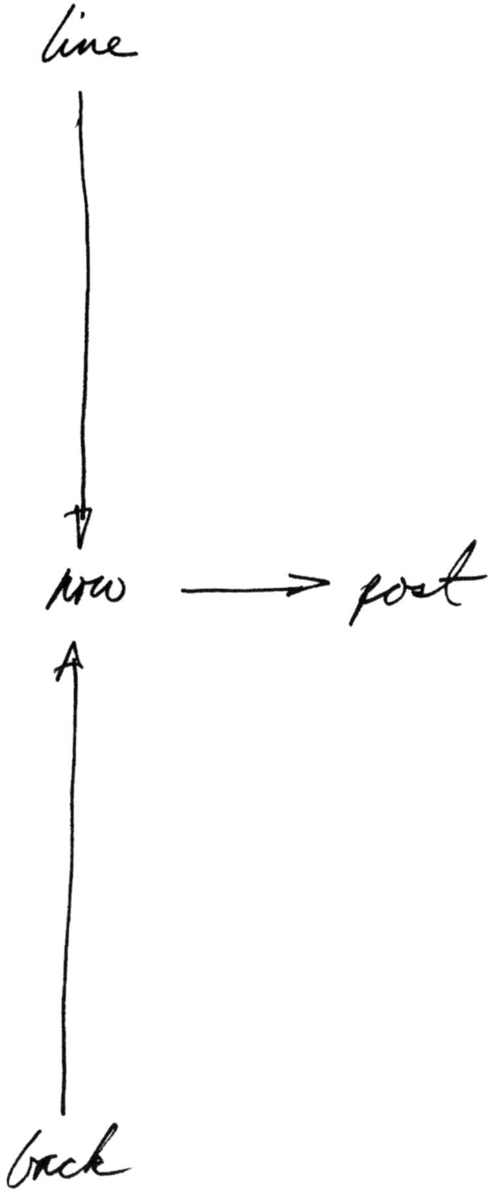
line
now
post
back

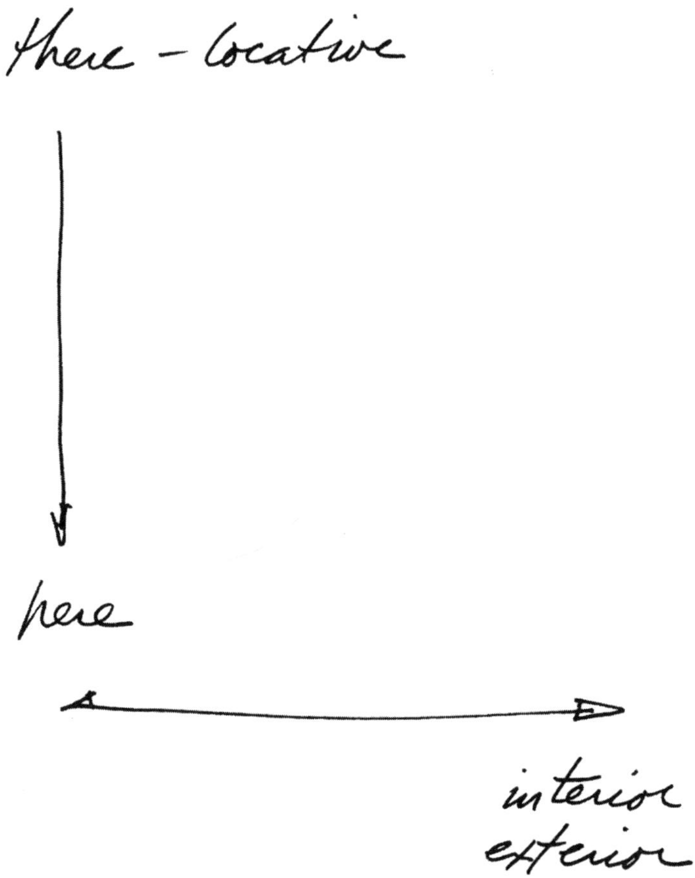
there - locative
here
interior
exterior

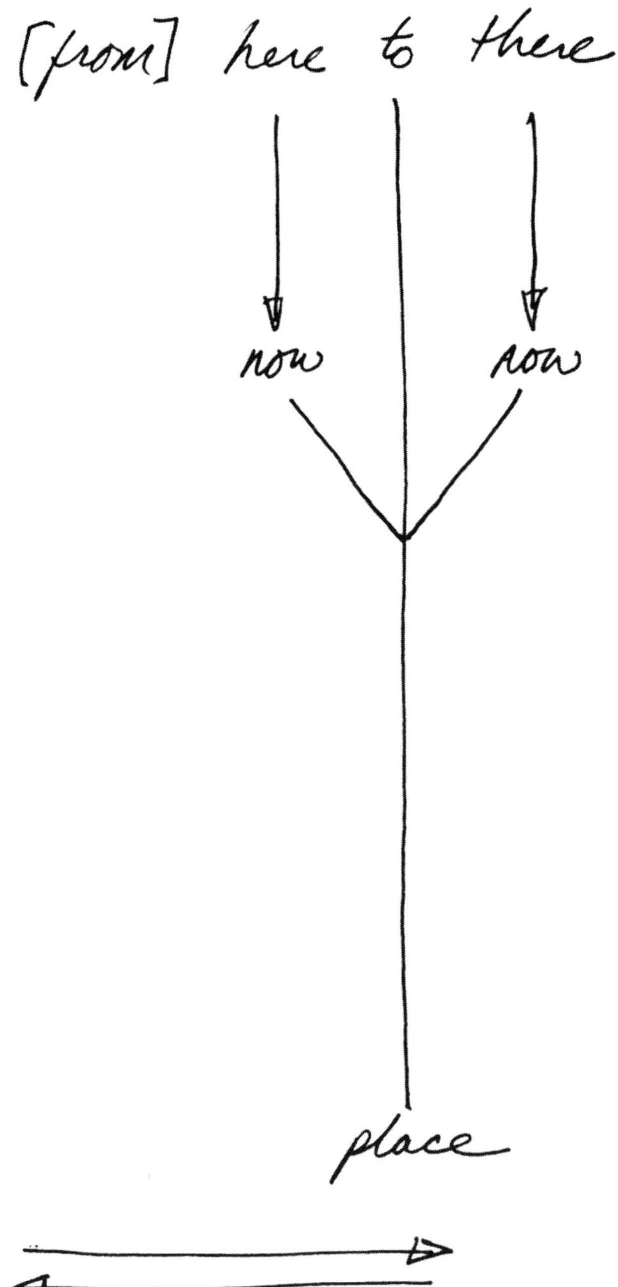
[from] here to there
now
now
place